The Rest

Ryan J. Torres

The Rest
Copyright ©2024 Ryan Torres
Cover- Kevin Durr

ISBN- 978-1-961043-03-9

Published by:

Blue Jade Press, LLC

Blue Jade Press, LLC
Vineland, NJ 08360
www.bluejadepress.com

For Pap: For the love and memories made
For Brigid: For the love and memories to come

And to the writings of the past and how a voice, and a life,
can grow and change

Table of Contents

How to Love Her   1
Car Seat   3
Outdoors   4
Hunter   5
Fight or Flight   6
To Be   7
That One Night   8
Easter Sunday   9
A Night Torn Mad by Poetry   10
Murphy   11
Quiet. Friday.   12
A Man on Fire   14
Frail   16
Gummy Bears   17
Trepidation   18
Income   19
When I Speak of Love   20
3%   21
Jimmy Hits the Slopes and Comes to Rest   22
Experience Life   24
Blue Heron   25
Ser   27
The Rotting Groom   28
How Do You Soften a Heart   30
The Miscarriage   32
Sadder than Hemingway's Baby Shoes   38
An Introvert's Contradiction   39
Love in the Time of Coronavirus   40
Hazard Pay   42
Insomnia During Quarantine   43
Corona Sutra   44
Hope for the Hopeless   46

Reminiscent	49
Essential Worker	51
Marketing Scheme	53
Definition of Hell	55
Face Mask	56
This Old House	58
Quarantine Inspiration Blues	60
Months Indoors	62
The Baby's Room	64
Meaning	68
Nothing Short of Love	69
To: The Ice Cream Truck Parked Outside of the Liquor Store	73
Post-Mortem Tea Leaves	75
The Day Batman Died	75
Elliot's Cannon Fodder	77
Gentle Workflow	79
Father's Day	81
Paddy Boy	83
Rat Salad	86
Disney at the Diner	88
The First Day of Spring; the Last of Phelps Sr.	90
Women and the Blues	93
Her Dress	95
The Beach	98
Kent	100
King Dick	102
Epiphany	103
The Commercialized Self	105
Contemplation	107
Art of the Self	109
Sleep	110
The Scream	112
Gizwald	113

Nightmare	115
For Aged Poets	119
Hurricane	121
Lamp Lighter	124
War	126
Marriage: Side "B"	128
Familiar	130
Write Right	131
Closing the House	132
Nature Writing	134
Five Minutes	136
Pickled	138
Masked	139
Camera Roll	140
Parenthood	141
Wanting Relief	142
Dear Katie,	143
Cereal Killer	144
Oak	145

How to Love Her

When you love her
(if you find yourself brave enough)
do so completely
you must help her wash away
all the things that came before
the stains that the others have left behind
imprints that you must kiss away
moments in the dark
that glide past each caress

When you love her
do so for both of you
do so for all of us
love fully
all of it for her

When you love her
lose yourself
the scars she has run deep
but, the river she runs to is deeper
I see her clothes
she sheds them for freedom
shed yours for her

When you love her
keep lilies on the kitchen table
let them wilt long enough
she will change the water
when it dirties
she knows her duty

Know yours

That's how to love her

Car Seat

How soon we forget
the things lost under car seats
like they still matter

Outdoors

When spring comes my way
typewriters won't slide around
out in the long grass

Hunter

Feels like I spent life
hunting sorrow and joy
they call it a poem

Fight or Flight

My beautiful brow
I have a terrible poker face
back up or throw down

To Be

Think of it this way
existence is bravery
it's not for cowards

That One Night

There was that night
that one night
when I sat in the living room
scotch in hand
and wondered
why in the hell
I made this pact
a long time ago

The deal
to push the keys
and beat this machine
with prose
and to never quit

Even when I wanted to
even when I really wanted to
even as I sat there telling myself
that I was done

Only to walk upstairs
sit at my desk
and write this

It was safe in the dark
sure, I was depressed
but I was safe
in that moment

But now there's this
and it always comes back
to this

Easter Sunday

Little kids
find plastic eggs
brightly colored
in the lawn
each filled with chocolate
they are told
a rabbit had left them
meanwhile
old ladies
in their Sunday best
drive extra slow
down our road
coming to a more-than-complete stop
at the sign
they are going to celebrate
the guest of honor
but nobody
wants to meet him

A Night Torn Mad by Poetry

Ripped and shredded to bits
this social situation ruined
fighting with the woman
inspired as all hell
with a dead cell phone battery
hours away from going home
in the middle of dinner
my scotch is almost gone
everyone else is sloshed
and here comes my water to nurse

Torres,
I can feel the magic leaving you

Torres,
I can feel the magic leaving you

Torres,
She's going to want to argue
about how weird you acted at dinner,
when the words were right there in front

Torres,
never forget your notebook at home
ever again

Murphy

I was given
a chair
from Princeton University
blood upholstery
with sturdy oak legs

I call it "The Brooding Chair"

When I received it
the first thing it taught me
was to sit
and plan the attack
and how sometimes
thinking
can be more productive
than writing

When I sit in it
I can only escape the world
small moments at a time

I know that I am only between poems
when I'm sitting there

Quiet. Friday.

You have had enough
and I can feel it.
You didn't work Friday night.
I don't blame ya.

You wanna be broke
or unhappy?
When I got home from my night shift
I told you about how
I ran over a pylon in the parking lot.
You stared past me.
I don't blame ya.

On the counter
in the kitchen
there were bottles of wine
and whiskey
and hard cider.
You were on a mission
and you extended your invitation
with libations.

For you,
cracking that cork
to celebrate yourself
was months in the making.
You wanted nothing to do with me.
I provided some frustrations too.
So I don't blame ya.

I'll pour this over two ice cubes
while you
chill out.

A Man on Fire

Virginia Woolf
taught me
that writing about a life
and every dew drop
of human existence
is no easy feat

Keep it ridiculous
keep it funny
keep it raw
give as much danger
as compassion

My love
taught me
the importance of reading
obituaries
on Sunday mornings

I can smell smoke
as I sit here
fully grown
yet not quite
laughing heart almost full
because it has been nothing
but smiles
between the funerals

I would like to write this man's book
his memoir
his biography
but, he won't let me just yet

He still thinks there's time left
his laughing heart isn't quite filled
he's still reading the obituaries
he is gathering kindling
his black suit is at the dry cleaners

There's another funeral
in the morning

Frail

Vertebrae shows through
a black dress
long legs crossed to cover
six-inch shin scar
the stomach gets pulled in
before she sits

Hold it

Don't breathe

Colored hair and makeup
hiding in plain sight

Socialite camouflage

Gummy Bears

One packet of gummy bears
with a note that read:
"Thank you so much for doing that. I love you. Xoxo"

One packet of gummy bears
my favorite candy
tacked to the corkboard in my office
with a thumbtack
next to your mother's obituary

One pack of gummy bears
the kind your mother would always buy
for me as well
and how I'd eat them
with complete enjoyment

One packet of gummy bears
the packet I got the day after
I carried your mother's casket
the same packet that continues
to stick to the corkboard

I failed to mention
that sharing them with her
was the best thing about them

Trepidation

Scared?
A bit…
Sensitive?
Just enough…
In tune, if you will
the fear
is that
I
will become
all
that I have hated
and if there isn't pause
for concern there
I don't know where
it would lie

Income

Funny
how much more an oil change costs
and how all you get
are ads for whiskey
and hobbies
on social media
and how it's always time
for the last heating bill
or the car needs inspected
or an increase in rent
or your cousin needs cash
or your uncle needs cash
or the dog needs to go to the vet
or you leave all the lights in the house on
and the electric bill goes through the roof
and how it all happens
right after
you get
your tax
return

When I Speak of Love

What I mean
when I speak of love
is that
when it ends
I want it to kill me
savoring every moment
in and out
of you
and our life together
the passionate embrace after the fight
the subtleness of your kiss
your hug
your playful wink
I want it to spell murder when it ends
I want to love completely
so that life ends completely
when it is done

I want the same for the rest
of you

3%

The iPad was at three percent
when I sat down to write this
I felt as though
I, too
was at 3%

It had been a hell of a day
and I didn't let it stop me.
so I put on Beethoven's "Silence"
and let the battery die

Knowing full well
that after it reached
perfect zero
we would both need
to recharge

Jimmy Hits the Slopes and Comes to Rest

"I use-ta sled down these hills
when I was a kid."
He told me many years ago.
"And in the spring,
the hills were covered with flowers.
Now it's all gravestones."

I liked to picture him
mounting his sled

Young Jimmy

Many years before he was
my grandfather

Catching speed and flying
the world his to pass for once
feeling the breeze and chill
savoring childhood,
and then coming to a stop
at the bottom
catching his breath
and shivering there
at the spot
where he would be buried
years later
by me

Now, the fresh flowers
no longer grow
among the tombstones
as I leave them in his wake

Experience Life

It's true you could try
almost anything one time
but first could mean last

Blue Heron

I was walking my dogs in the park
it was overcast and grey
between bouts with the storm.
passing two people
who didn't acknowledge my "hello"
and preferred their phones
and *Pokémon Go*

Then,
she emerged

The blue heron
swooping like an autumn leaf
gliding on the strong wind.
and landing in the lake

Each hesitant on the next move

And their Pokémon
never noticed

Ser

In Spanish,
it is simply a means to be
that is, you.
Ser
makes me think
of Abram,
before God gave him his "real name"
and made him the father of the word

Seri — her name

Not yet Sarah
mother of the word
being walked into Egypt
in a city of hungry dogs
with her beauty
cascading off every hard surface
"Just pretend you're my sister,
that way I can protect myself
from the men who would kill me
to make you their own."

But I
am a better man
regarding your beauty
these are my words
"You are the most beautiful thing
I have ever seen."

The city's dogs are outside
I hear them crying at night
love is a worthy fight
You are far too pretty
to be my sister

The Rotting Groom

Katie,
I'm under your window
beneath the dying leaves
where you buried me in October rust
on that beautiful Halloween

Katie,
I'm moving soil
amongst the worms and crawling things
to remove myself from this autumn grave
to show you the love I bring

Katie,
I'm crossing the porch boards
the ones I repaired and stained
to come inside our loving home
the one we built and named

Katie,
Im crossing the threshold
the moon it lights the doorway
the one I carried you over
on our very wedding day

Katie,
I'm coming up the stairs
the ones you pushed me down
before burying me in the garden tomb
adorned by wisteria crowns

Katie,
I'm outside your bedroom
the same that we lovingly shared
I'm still dreaming of those passionate moments
that left us exhausted and bare

Katie,
I'm at your bedside
you turn and coo in slumber
I've come to claim you finally
and together we'll both go under

Katie,
Can you taste the soil?
the rot of eons now beckon you
come lay down in this new bed, my love.
there's plenty of room for two

How Do You Soften a Heart?

How do you soften a heart?
Have you studied enough poetry?
Hell—
Have you written enough poetry?
Felt enough poetry?
Seen, smelled, tasted?

What softens a heart?
It is easier to break an ego
than it is to soften the hardhearted
beat an ego in contest
correct it in good company
don't give it the respect it so desperately needs
and it will break

But how do you soften a heart?
Well, how does it harden?
Has it been wracked by tragedy?
Does it know what loss tastes like?

Is it bitter?
Were its dreams dashed upon the rocks of reality?
Did it give up before the journey began?
Does it live with regret?
Does it hate?
Is it lonely?
Is time alone its mistress or master?
Has it bent its knee before the chaos of nature?
Does it not know that flowers bloom on battlefields too?

How do you soften a heart?
Kindness

kindness chisels at the stonework.
kindness is a start

Hope.
hope will open the locked doors
and gates.
hope will not turn back the clock
but it will draw open the shades
it will let the light in.
it will let love know
that someone is home.

Love.
imagine filling every void with it
imagine a heart
brimming with it

So
How do you soften a heart
like you have softened mine?

The Miscarriage

1.
Crisp autumn morning.
You put the pregnancy test in my hand
in the living room
and say "You ready for round two, Torres?"

I was
I really was

2.
9 weeks in and I get an ultrasound photo.
a small bump in black and white.
pure and innocent
with the words "Hi Dad"
in the center of the little body

3.
We tell your parents, and I tell a coworker
her mother crocheted a hat and coat
for the newborn
your parents were awestruck by the news
of a second coming.

4.
I remember you saying
"Something doesn't feel right."
I remember thinking it was because
you were just carrying a son this time

You were right.

5.
You spotted in the morning
then, at the 21-week appointment
you got your answer
I was teaching first period when the phone rang.
you cried hard sobs of despair into my ear.
I don't remember leaving work
I just did

6.
He died just after 9 weeks.
my wife was a heap on the couch for the first few hours
we were driving our daughter home from
your parents' house
when you felt a cramp, and a flow
You began to bleed.
Your body had realized that it was feeding
something that would never eat

7.
My daughter is watching Bluey and eating snacks
as you are hemorrhaging upstairs.
I'm running back and forth
between two completely different atmospheres
as you call for towels and bleed through two pairs of pants
I say, "If you don't leave for the hospital now,
I'm calling 911."

You wrap a towel around your waste and leave.

8.
When your mother arrives
to watch our daughter
I leave.

I'm hoping I don't find you in a ditch
on the side of the road.
but you made it.
and I make it
and we are in the E.R.

9.
Seven hours.
seven hours of scraping,
and wincing, and pain
I am watching from the corner
like a sadistic fly
You wonder where the baby could be.
The dumpster? The car? The grocery bag in the kitchen
trash can? The septic tank?
I caught you twice while you were fainting
I laid you on a bed covered in blood
Now blood is all I see

10.
We got home at 1 a.m.
You stayed up and talked with your mom
while I called off of work
I begin cleaning the blood off the bathroom tile
I take a shower
healthy water mixes with fresh tears

11.
The first night of sleep
I dreamt that I was holding you
a small, lifeless form yearning for the fire of life
some small spark of possibility
I tried to breathe life into you
I fail again and again

12.
I'm being a good dad to a gifted child
one who is oblivious to the fact
that her mother almost bled to death.

We contemplated sending a 'thank you' card
to the ER nurse

Danielle, if you're reading this:
We love you.
Thank you for taking such good care of us.

13.
I keep seeing blood.
I keep seeing them scrap the cold metal inside of you.
I keep seeing large chunks of tissue.
I keep seeing the steady stream of viscera
from that beautiful opening
one same that I watched my daughter
spring forth from.

I keep seeing blood.

I've been seeing it since.

14.
I don't really remember the month of November
Mostly small details, and
how they can mean so much to a life
I became hyper-focused on the basic needs to sustain life
snuggling my daughter
reading an extra book at bedtime.

Watching her eat
and drink,
and sleep.
and watching my wife eat,
and drink,
and sleep.
and how I would tell myself
that these are good things.
they are beautiful and necessary.
I had to keep telling myself
that I'm a good father.
these things happen.
the "nature" of nature is chaos.

Complete and absolutely beautiful chaos

I'm thankful it wasn't worse.
but I miss the son I never met

15.
The blood test results came back
he was positive for down syndrome
Down syndrome babies are so cute
they grow up to be so wholesome
and fun loving.
I would have taken you in any form

16.
My wife is staring at the bassinet in our room
she is staring at her bathroom floor
she is staring at the changing table

I started remodeling the bathroom

17.
Somewhere in all this we had Thanksgiving…

18.
It hit me, finally
the reality of my grief
now I am low

We are closing in on Christmas.

The bathroom is done.
we get Covid.
I've missed a lot of work.

Oh, well.

19.
I take the toolbox back upstairs to the bedroom
you ask what I am doing.
I'm going to take the changing table and the bassinet apart
I'm going to put them in the attic to collect dust

You have gotten back from therapy.

You stop me in the hallway.
"No," you say.
I want to get through this.
I want to try again.

Do you?

20.
…Yes.
Yes, I do.

Sadder than Hemingway's Baby Shoes

An ad on Etsy
for tree of life
baby urns
urging me to act quickly
apparently they are selling fast

An Introvert's Contradiction
(a COVID Lament)

I'd like to tell myself
selfishly
(of course)
that I'll come out the other side
of this
a better writer
or lover,
or fisherman,
or dreamer,
or underwear cleaner
but the truth is that
(so far)
I've come to the conclusion
that I might come out softer
Maybe,
(dare I say),
a little less broody
and a bit less moody
and it's all because
I miss you
so damn much

Love in the Time of Coronavirus

Fifteen pounds of potatoes
three bags of coffee
160 pounds of dog food
assorted cans of beans, tuna, and chicken
a stocked freezer
and a second fridge full of beer and hard cider

"I think we'll last a week"

I remember you saying
"It's all going to collapse"
and that you "hoped"
that "it never goes back to the way it was"

People are now living
the way that I preferred to spend my childhood

People's concerns for each other
bring me hope

The way people are realizing that their politicians
aren't who they say they are
brings me hope

The old woman eating lunch alone at the park
because the first day of spring
wasn't going to hold her back
(just six feet apart)
brings me hope

The animals that I have seen by the creek
out my back window
bring me everything else

They were waiting for us
to ground ourselves
and see what was really important
before the world lets us out again

How calm we are in this house
in the face of infection
makes life more beautiful in a special way

May we never wash our hands
of that

Hazard Pay

They want to walk the line
between keeping an economy,
and keeping a virus at bay.

You've already got us
repressed,
and recessed,
and depressed.

We cannot eat the money.

Can't inject the bills
and ask COVID to pay the rent.

We are learning first hand
about how useless the money is
when
you
can't
breathe.

Insomnia During Quarantine

Sleeping is the worst
during this time

I keep dreaming
that armed illiterates
break into my house,
shoot my dogs,
and steal my toilet paper

None of them stand 6-feet apart
None of them wear masks
None of them wear gloves

All the president's men…

I hope
this isn't
foreshadowing

Corona Sutra

Sex during a pandemic
is like being in a Jacuzzi tub
surrounded by lit candles
and the lavender aroma
of the bubbles
the temperature is perfect
you don't have to recoil your nethers
and wince before fully submerging

It feels perfect

And then someone else enters…
and water-boards you

We fuck like our lives depend on it
like we are on a burning ship
(because we are)

When your hot breath hits my face,
I refuse to reach for my N95

We don't make out like we usually do
it seems too dangerous now

Kissing has become a stigma

One of us deserves a good night's sleep

You, my love,
have been deemed "essential"
other people are relying on you
for healthcare

The least I can do
is give you an orgasm

Hope for the Hopeless

They ask me to take them out
and show them
the spot
where love died

I am a carpenter without a hammer
I am a writer with a loss of words.
I am the sunlight through a cracked window
as it lands on the carpet,
illuminating the dog hair

I am spending a lot of time
during this pandemic
walking around the house
drinking from old bottles
All of these bottles
are from happier times

Yet, I cannot taste those times
in the inebriation

They taste like longing

They ask me to take them out
and show them
the spot
where love died

I have an impression in my beard
from my face masks.
I now look like the Man in the Moon
I have a swollen belly
from ciders and comfort foods,
but my back and legs are strong
from pulling weeds and invasive saplings.
my fingertips hurt from the typewriter

I'm grateful

But still
they ask me to take them out
and show them
the spot
where love died

So, I'll take them out
and I will show them the holes in the house
where the birds have made nests
I'll show them the bees
high on nectar
as they dance from flower to flower
I'll show them the broken boards on the front porch

I will tell them
that love has not died
It's hiding,
sleeping,
resting,
and waiting
for us

Now,
I am a carpenter with a new hammer.
I am a writer with his words.
I am not the cracked window
or the sunlight
I am
simply
illuminated

Reminiscent

Remember getting a drink with your buddy
after a rough day
or a fight with the better half?

Remember going to the ballpark
with your old man?

Remember visiting your grandparents
without worrying about whether or not
it would result
in unintentional
manslaughter?

Remember hugging your buddies,
homies,
friends,
comrades,
and even some strangers?

Remember shaking hands?

Remember shaking your ass on a crowded dance floor?

Remember the unmasked face?

Remember when you didn't have to question
every cough?

Remember going out to lunch
then walking around the shops
and touching everything
but buying absolutely nothing?

Hell, remember arguments
and feeling the angry finger in your chest?

Remember the delicate
and rare flower
of a kiss?

I do
I do
Yeah
I sure do

Essential Worker

Every day
you arrive to your post
and load your immune system
with vitamin C
tumeric
and ginger

You hand out healthcare
like prizes

The children need you

When you arrive
they take your temperature
you always run a little cold

Then they fit you
with your landmine shoes
and you gracefully walk
from room to room
and learn who became sick
sometime during the night

When you get home
you strip naked
and throw your clothes into the washer
you leave your shoes on the porch

Then you shower
then you towel off
then you dress
and then, you say "Hello"

You hate how the mask
makes your face break out
with fresh pimples

You never worry about catching it

At night
you drink Sleepytime tea
and take melatonin
still, you toss and turn

The only thing
you fear
is getting me sick

The only thing
I fear
is you getting sick

Now,
who said
that only children
were selfish
and vain?

Marketing Scheme

The commercials have all changed their tunes
All the online shops sell masks
of all kinds
yet, your cousin's wife makes
the best ones
out of love and worry

Wells Fargo
wants me to know
that they are here for me
during this trying time
But, when I call and ask for help
with the rent and bills,
the automated voice
laughs.

Kellogg's wants me to know
that their cereal
will help me relax
and stop worrying about my grandparents
and my best friend with Cystic Fibrosis.

I want Kellogg's to know
that the only reason they exist
is because their founder
hated masturbating so much
that you should feed your children
his crunchy, bland, tasteless
breakfast cereal

And to the rest of you:
I'm not giving you any of the money
that I don't have,
for stuff
that I don't need

Haven't you learned?

Capitalism
and consumerism
don't cure a damn thing

The longer we stay home
during COVID,
the closer you come
to living
and dying
like the rest
of us

Definition of Hell

Hell is the lack of an imagination.
Hell is other people.
Hell is missing other people.
Hell is wondering if your essential loved ones will get sick.
Hell is anxiety over who you might have killed at the
  grocery store.
Hell is waiting.
Hell is boredom.
Hell is wasted time.
Hell is depression.
Hell is when no one wears a face mask.
Hell is when no one moves away from you as you
  walk the dog.
Hell is not spending that quality time with your elders.
Hell is not having access to a computer or internet.
Hell is a dead cell phone battery.
Hell is a sink full of dirty dishes.
Hell is the amount of time spent cleaning the house.
Hell is the amount of time-spent clearing the litter box.
Hell is not after life.
Hell is current.
Hell can be beaten
Because none of us deserve it.
Hell is a social construct.
Hell is a control mechanism.
Hell exists inside.
It makes me wonder:
What the hell?

Face Mask

I'm sorry.
I forgot to wear my facemask.
You followed me to the mechanic's shop
for my left headlight
and an oil change.
I had to grab their pen.
I had to grab their paper
from the fold-down compartment
that all the customers use.
I filled it out as quick as I could.
No one was around.
My facemask down
around my neck.

When I went to feed the slot,
the mechanic came out of the building
with a facemask on.

He scared me.
I didn't know anyone was in there.

So I handed him my key
from a full arm's length away.

His conversation about the car:
simple
hurried
and awkward.
(Like always)

I got into your car
and you told me about myself.

I forgot to pull my facemask up.
I felt diseased and sorry.
You reassured my paranoia.
I felt like I threw my whole life away.

It's been three months
of perfection
until today.

I'll never forget again.

Corona has no chance
against your wrath.

This Old House

Since I've become a homebody
(no complaints here)
I took the hot-blooded man route
and began doing minor renovations
around the house and the grounds

Weeding, trimming,
hammering, screwing,
sanding, staining,
fixing...

I google what to do half the time
and just give it a shot

Not so useless after all...

But it wasn't what I learned
that has kept me intrigued,
it's what I noticed

This house breathes

It has a pulse

Its lights flicker
and the breeze
that wafts in from the open windows
pushes the ghosts right past you

It doesn't sleep when we do

It has hidden passages that connects
areas to other areas

It feels like it's watching me,
but it feels welcoming,

for now...

Quarantine Inspiration Blues

I couldn't sleep
so, I joined the cat during her midnight prowl
of the downstairs
I contemplated whether or not
I should make chocolate chip cookies
at two in the morning,
simply because I was hungry for one

My wife was asleep
when I took a bath in Epson salts
that promised me relaxation
but the scotch and water
in the mason jar
had different plans

I tried to go to bed at one point
the eldest dog
took my place
her head on my pillow
that majestic and sleepy
"fuck you, I'm not moving"
look on her face
as I turned off the lamp
and made my exit

I checked in on active people
fellow night birds
on social media

I folded laundry
did the dishes
watched T.V.

3 a.m.
nothing...

So I went into my office
after setting down Voltaire
and wrote out this poem

How are you sleeping these days?

Months Indoors

I left the house about
five times
in the first two months
of the pandemic
that's a lot of time to spend indoors
but at least,
now, I know I have the blood
for solitary confinement

If someone would have told me
before all of this
that I would need is one month
to get over anxiety enough
to write a poem,
I would have dry heaved laughter
into their face

But, they would have not been wrong

I'm glad that you come home to me my love
I'm glad that we don't live
in that one-bedroom apartment anymore.
The cops were always knocking at the door
and the schizophrenic neighbor
played "Psycho Killer"
til 3 a.m.

Could you imagine being stuck there now?

I have books,
but, never read as much as I would like
I have video games,
but, don't play them that much
there's online Dungeons and Dragons
but, that online happens on weekends
there's cleaning the house
and mowing
and raking
and petting the dogs
and the cat (but not for long)
and the rabbit

My mother-in-law brought us groceries
on Saturday afternoons for a while
because my wife had been exposed at work
but never developed symptoms or sickness

I think my day drinking scares it away
I think our love-making scares it away
I think that it thinks
"Holy shit. If I infect that guy
I'll be too close to that brain for comfort
and I'll just create my own vaccine."

It's hard for a beast to come at night
when the generous host has been staying up too
anticipating the same kind of chaos
we both crave

The Baby's Room

We got pregnant
during a global pandemic
because we were ready
even though the world was not

The paradise we found
was in the moments
we got to enjoy those months
together

The baby's room
will be where your dressing room was

We chose the cream color for the walls
and the green color for the trim

I began painting the room
while my grandfather
died of COVID-19
in Hershey, Pennsylvania

We used to go up there to the park
and chocolate world,
and to eat at restaurants

But I'll never go there again
I have no reason to

The last time we went up there
we went to the outlet stores
and got some coffee
and just talked

We always just talked and laughed

Every Saturday, it was he and I
my allowance
and the arcade
or the old fishing hole at Stover's Park
or the movies
or walking around the mall
or we'd just sit in the living room
and watch cartoons

I'd talk about writing something
something great.
something that people would like to read.
and even though others would ask "why?"
He'd say "go for it"

I'd paint a wall
I'd get too tired after teaching all day
I'd get hungry
or, I'd be over it
and I'd wash my hands
and my brush
and go downstairs to my
pregnant wife

I'd place my hand on her belly
and I'd feel my child kick

The two of you will never meet

Two months' shy
so close
yet so far

The next night
after work
I'd be up there painting again.
trying to make something beautiful in the moment

Both of us alone in white rooms
each working towards a different goal

I'll call my mother
your daughter
I'll call my grandmother (nan)
your wife

They will be in shambles
they will beg me to come to them,
I will say all the phrases synonymous with "No"
because we are in a pandemic
the only thing that keeps everyone safe
is to be apart

The only thing that I wanna do
is drive to Lebanon, Pennsylvania
and comfort them

And, then, drive to Hershey, Pennsylvania
and be with him

The unimaginable thing
is having the person I admire most,
the one whom is responsible for the survival
of my art
and my self
has to die
alone

The baby's room is finished

My wife likes the colors and so do I
we'll move the furniture in after the
baby shower

In the Spring,
my father and uncle will show up
and we'll work on the house
we'll get everything ready
for a new life

And though you would not be here
as the child grows,
I will carry your laughter
through these new memories
as you have planted it
in mine

Long after the paint
is dry and
you've turned out the lights
and closed the door

Meaning

Life is the epitome of

Survive this
Now survive this
Now survive this
Now this
And this
and don't forget this
until the day
you don't

Nothing Short of Love
Or, How I Learned to Stop Worrying and Love the Virus

1.

I have become humbled by tragedy.
Tragedy,
being the new normal.

I have become open to possibilities.
I'm told they are endless.

I've fallin' in love all over again.
With her
With life
With the future
With you

I've seen an act of kindness
so pure and so sweet
that I no longer doubt kindness.

I've seen resemblances in photos.
You and I looked the same in 10th grade.
We both have the same sag to our bottom lip.

2.

The virus took you from me.
A light in the darkness extinguished.
You waited for permission to die.
So I gave it to you.
I beared your pall.
I spoke as eloquently as possible.
The ground was cold
20 degrees in February
and snow everywhere.
You would have laughed your ass off
and said "Is it cold enough for ya, big guy?"
I could feel your elbow in my ribs.
We both looked like smartasses in 10th grade.
I would have given you The Flowers of the
    Forest.
I would have given you the longest procession
this country had ever seen.
Yet, I would have traded it all
for one more Saturday together.

3.

I've anticipated new life
from this vantage point.
Painting
and putting the crib together,
as my wife strokes her belly
and you dance in her womb.

I've learned that god only exists
in the hearts and eyes
of women.

I've fallen in love with you
and your strength
over and over again.

I will be stronger for you
and for our child.

4.

Despite the fear
Despite the anxiety
Despite the distance
Despite the sorrow

I've learned to push love forward
to put it first in the fight

I've seen a darkness
and a goodness

And for all it has taken
for all the times it got in the way,
it only made us
more beautiful
in the end

To: The Ice Cream Truck Parked Outside of the Liquor Store

That's it.
That's the poem.

Post-Mortem Tea Leaves

I see your Constant Comment
those dried out husks of promise
begging for moisture
the tea bags the widow gave you
her dead husband's favorite tea

You have a habit
of attracting the leaves
of the deceased

But, unlike your grandmother,
(whom you've had tea with often
before she passed),
you've never had a cup
with him

However, you have borne witness
to the vodka
he poured
room temperature
into a pint glass and drained
without a wince

Surprising to find out
he even liked tea
at all

The Day Batman Died
(For Adam West)

On the day Gotham lost its hero
I was debating between mac and cheese
and potato salad
at a picnic

On the morning The Caped Crusader fell
I hung up my 1989
Michael Keaton
BATMAN
action figure.
the first one ToyBiz ever made

I hung it on the wall
behind the door
I wanted him to watch from the shadows
as you drew your last breaths

It wasn't the Penguin
It wasn't Riddler
It was Freeze or Ivy
It wasn't even the Joker

It was leukemia

The battle within
eventually triumphs
even when it comes to
the dark knight
I imagine that the bat cave is quiet
now.

Goodnight Batmobile

Goodnight Alfred

Goodnight Robin

Goodnight commissioner Gordon

Goodnight shark repellent and grappling hook

Goodnight cape and cowl

And goodnight Bat signal

"Shut it down. He's not coming."

Elliot's Cannon Fodder

I feel like Prufrock
when I put missed opportunities
in front
of the hard work
being poured into the present
and how much
it would pay off
in the future

I could have it all
but I would have to stop thinking
in my usual damning way

I cannot afford
to be at the bottom of the stairs
and worried about the climb

Let the women come
and go

Why interrupt their
conversations
about other artists?

I can't afford
to keep combing over
thinning hair

I'll shave it
when it gets too thin
and count it as one less thing
that will catch fire
while walking through the flames
of this life

It's not about how many times
you have to measure out the coffee
it's how good
each cup tastes

Sometimes
the simplest poem
helps one
cope
the most

Especially
when one
is being fooled
by their youth

Gentle Workflow

It's spring and I just want to walk somewhere
but, I can wait
I've waited this long

Work will always be work,
no matter what
that's how it got its name

Make the workdays lively
keep fresh fruit on the shelf
next to your desk

My office smells
like orange rinds
and strong black coffee
I should collect flowers
or fig leaves
and keep them in a purple vase

Every once in a while
there is a secret poem
when everything is still

It's still spring
when I'm not at work
I sit at the breakfast table
reading Lawrence
wondering where all the beauty comes from
and why it goes away so quickly

Back home
away from the labor
my apartment smells like sandalwood
and even stronger coffee
and there are flowers
that she gathers for me
they stay pretty, even when wilted

There is also a place for that poem

Father's Day

We both woke up at a decent time
so I decided to take him out
for Father's Day

We went to a dive
on the edge of town
for a typical breakfast
in a typical atmosphere

Neither of us could find anything to talk about.

We ate our eggs
We ate our toast
I had a fruit cup
He had bacon
We had coffee and water,
He would stare at the hostess
I would stare out the window

"You look like you've lost weight,"
he said.

"Twelve pounds since I moved back to town,"
I replied.

 "You need to run though.
You can't just lift and diet.
You need to run.
Suck it up and run one mile
every now and then."

I've always hated running…

We finished our breakfasts
and I paid

The girl at the register
who had been around my age
smiled and raised an eyebrow at me.
But I didn't notice
not the way he did.

"You could have had her,"
he told me as we crossed the parking lot
"Maybe she's a runner"

Paddy Boy

Like one hand clapping
in a darkened theater
to the swan's song
Patrick
sits at home
alone,
and fights his disease
for as long as he can

The empty house—
            far from the streets of Dublin—
has a hint of ghostly cigarette smoke
from tobacco long since punched out,
that is seeping out of the wood floor
and paneling

His kitchen
is barren
except for a loaf of white bread
and a teapot that is whistling

There is a transparent television
he bought for his son,
who is now in prison

As Patrick walks around
he gently grabs the back of chairs
and the tabletops
with hands calloused
from years of rebel wars,
and masonry

His dog
Molly
the gentle boxer
doesn't bark at strangers
and never leaves his side

"She sleeps nex' ta me in da bed,"
he says in a sweet brogue

She's all he has now
his sons never call
and his ex-wife has all the money

They gave him experimental drugs
and told him
that he could have ten years left
if he takes them every day
they are still
in the bag
from the pharmacy

The P.O.W. experiences
were recess
the brain tumor
was a flesh wound
the psych ward
was a vacation

The toe amputation
was a tickle

Leukemia
could be different

"It's not dyin' tha scares meh,"
he says
"It's bein' alone
while ah do it"

Molly cups his hand
between her paws
and licks his fingertips
as steam rises from the teacup

Rat Salad

What do two
blind
female
albino
rats
dream about
when they sleep Siamese
in a cheetah print hammock
on the top floor
of their
habitat?

Do they dream
of perfect vision
through piercing
strawberry
jelly bean
eyes?

Viewing the world
around them
as a shag carpet
panorama

I bet
they don't waste one second
dreaming about an office
and a computer screen
and running the corporate wheel
as soda cans crack

and asses get fatter,
and how "How may I direct your call"
echoes through the corridors

I hope that they only dream
of their caretaker's baby talk
through the comforting darkness,
as perfect pink noses
find a never-ending
feast

Disney at the Diner

I remember being nine
and I remember reaching
for my father's wedding ring
under a booth
at the diner

I remember reaching
past the chicken bone
as they argued in heated whispers

Past the broken canyons and straw wrappers
as he complained

Over the chewing gum
and around the fork
as she refused to back down

To grab a piece
of gold
twinkling
in the darkness

I remember reaching
as the tired-eyed waitress
began to vacuuming
two booths down

She must have seen
my worn sneakers
and chubby legs
sticking out
from underneath
where I was reaching

To save my perception
of a normal
family
life

Because I was raised
on delusions of grandeur,
as Disney characters
sang me to sleep,
and the good guys
always won

That's what I was reaching for

I was Indiana Jones
when I gave that ring back to him,
and he put it on for good

I was Luke Skywalker.

I was Buzz Light-Year.

And I. Was. Batman.

And we were going home.
because everything loved
is worth the reach

The First Day of Spring;
the Last of Phelps Sr.

The long winter finally died
as you breathed your last
through hospice tubes,
and the earth opened her mouth
to turn your death
into a million blades
of grass

Did the nurse hesitate about
whether or not
to let you have
the medicine that numbs the pain?

Or,
did she almost let you feel this last bit
for those families
burdened and mocked
while they mourned,
as you
and your children
waved signs,
claiming a higher power
demanded it

Exclaiming
"GOD HATES…"
"GOD HATES…"

Well, there are those who now chant back in silence—
but will not picket—
because we can now keep moving forward,
now that your wall of spite
has fallen

The believers chanting:
"God does not hate."

The non-believer chanting:
"We do not hate."

The true-believer chanting:
"We know how to love."

The first day of spring was cloudy,
but it was pure

And you couldn't enjoy it

I have but one god

You've never met her...

She is My Lady of Perpetual Astonishment

She leads me to fresh ink
and smooth pages,
so that I can drink from the elixir
of this life
I am her vessel

She moved me
when the news broke
about your death

She thought you were worthy
of at least
one poem

I cannot say
that she and I
always see
eye to eye

But we,
like the rest of humanity,
are growing to understand
that it is our differences that make us beautiful

Why couldn't you have planted a garden
instead?

Women and the Blues

Lightening Hopkins
and Taj Mahal
had the strings

But only women
know how to sing
the blues

You can catch the Katy
but, have you ever listened to her cry?

It doesn't matter who the conductor is
or how many times the rain
on the main drag
reminds you of her

It seems
that women were born
to sing the blues

She's there
to take the madness
from your life,
and carry it
with her

Whether you're 2,000 miles away
or two steps from the door
she will sing the blues

And when you finally
realize this,
do yourself a favor
and listen
until the song is over

Her Dress

"Hang on," she said.

Her phone lands
on a soft surface,
muffling the receiver

A minute passes slowly

I hear the phone
catch the air
and crackle
as it is retrieved

"Sorry," she said.
"I was taking off my dress"

Oh

"Which one,"
I asked

"The black one," she said.
"The one you think is ugly"

Nonsense

I remember that dress
just like I remember
all the other dresses
especially,
how she used to take them off

The little white zipper
that got caught halfway down
but a slight tug
freed its tension

Freedom from the dress
was always pure relief
and as it fell to the floor,
it brought her back
to all natural.
her soft shoulders,
body,
and every tiny freckle,
that nature dripped onto her

A relief
from the mystery
of what she had on
underneath
with the pretty patterns
and colorful fabric

If there was anything
there at all

Every dress
special in its own way

Mixing with
the atmosphere
spilling over furniture
coloring the floor
or adding to the excitement

"Are you still there?"
she asked

The Beach

With my head in the clouds
my ass in a chair
and my feet buried
deep in sand

I breathe deep
and drift off
as waves crash
to the shore

I awoke
sometime later
to the sound of terrible pop music
and a child screaming

The beach was littered
with people

I watched them consume
and leave behind
carbon footprints

But before I slipped into
an existential crisis
I saw her

A maroon bikini
covered a thin body
and diamond earrings
clung to her earlobes

Her smile was pure pearl temptation

There wasn't a strand of hair
on her head

She played in the surf alone

A girl in her twenties with cancer
being admired by a boy in his twenties

I wanted her to have the beach

All of it

Forever

But we rarely get what we deserve

Kent

Clark,
you gotta help us, man.
It's been raining for days,
and the people are starting to drown
in their bedrooms.

Clark,
you gotta help me, man.
She has a new job
and the distance is making me hungry
for the taste of foreign salts.

Clark,
love the glasses, man.
Heard you lost some weight
and found some insanity.

Clark,
you gotta help her, man.
She ran into the city
and fell straight into the bottle.
All she does is work
and rarely smiles.
She goes on dating sites
just to read the profiles
of people who are sadder than she.
He's in prison til January.
And in turn, so is she.

You gotta help us,
Clark.
The spandex is a bit too much,
and the heat vision won't save us
from this winter.

I wish I was as strong as you.
I wish my heart was made of gold
instead of tin and ice.

I would have flown away years ago.

King Dick

The skeleton of Richard III
was found under a parking lot
and Elvis
died on the toilet

Long live the king

Epiphany

My father called it
the "Ah-ha" moment
because he didn't know
the word
"epiphany"

I don't think he's ever written poetry

But he said
that in Maine
while walking along the harbor,
the ship he stood next to
made him feel
like the head of a pin

      Small...
               Insignificant...

Until he climbed
the nearby hills
which loomed over harbor

The ship
became the pin

That was when
he measured himself
against the weight of the world

Then he proclaimed,
"Ah-ha"

I made my own proclamation
while standing on a beach

I was trying to determine
how many drops of water
formed the Atlantic,
while counting grains of sand
between my toes,
as thousands of blades of grass
waved in the breeze
amidst the tree next to the house

"Ah-ha"

"Ah-ha"
proclaimed Einstein
years before from a similar setting

"Is it better to be better than to be anything?"
I recited

"Are there any original thoughts left?"
Dad asked

"No.
Just clever plagiarism"

The Commercialized Self

I dwell inside
this commercialized self

An Interstate
start-and-go brain
floating in grape Kool-Aid
inside a peanut M&M skull

My body
is an organic
farm-raised
grass-fed
all vegetarian temple
that runs on Starbucks promises
with a Folger's budget

This commercialized self
bleeds fruit punch Gatorade
and secretes its childhood immunizations

In the summer,
I sweat Clorox
and Mobil oil

In the dead of winter
my breath against the cold
is a miasma of American Spirits

My dreams
are brought to you
by Lagavulin scotch and Royal

And, we will return you
to our regularly scheduled self
after these important messages

Stay tuned

Contemplation

Like watching paint dry, as
I sit around contemplating poetry

Contemplation
for the greater good

A good that is greater than myself

Contemplation
over other words and themes,
worlds and schemes
that,
in the end,
still may not amount
too much

Poetry will not change
the world

It will not teach you
how to raise
a child

It will not teach you
how to help
your fellow man,
or your fellow woman

It will not teach you
to coexist
perfectly

But still I sit here,
away from everything,
and contemplate

Art of the Self

If you're good,
they'll hate you.
If you suck,
they'll hate you.
If you follow the rules,
they'll hate you.
If you believe in yourself,
they'll hate you.
If you believe in nothing,
they'll hate you.
If you go far,
they'll hate you.
If you don't go at all,
they'll hate you.
If you practice your art,
they'll hate you.
If you perfect your art,
they will despise you.

Isn't it a relief
to know
that it isn't
about them?

Sleep

I was in bed
when the world ended

The city,
felt like miles beneath,
with burning street lights
like a million tiny suns,
suddenly dimmed;
then extinguished

In the time it takes
for you
to close your eyes

The hustle and bustle
of people,
taxis,
buses...

Silenced
Hushed

In the time it takes
for you
to place one side
of your head
against the mattress,
and compress the other
with a pillow
I was in bed
when the world finally ended

Felt like miles away,
in a place
where words don't string together

Where the hands of the clocks
all follow the hour
and yet time
finally ended

The Scream

All I want to do
is scream a little bit
into this typewriter

Punching the keys
hard,
and with so much precision,
that it would put a prize fighter
to shame

A scream

So loud,
with the art
of silence,
that it echoes
in the heart,
and lingers in the soul,
like a mad disease
with no cure

Screaming

Like a lunatic
at the harvest moon,
with poetry
ripe for the picking

Until the screaming
is over

For now,
at least...

And I can finally rest,
the page can stop crying,
the Royal
can stop smoking,
and the poor bastards
who took the time
to read,
or hear
my words,
can limp away
and lick their wounds

Gizwald

Have you seen little Gizwald puppy
go traipsing through the yard all night?
To all those who drive past and see,
he can produce an awful fright.

Little Gizwald puppy
is a sneaky, slippery thing.
Who no more frolics in the flowers,
or watches the mockingbirds sing.

Now, he is a monster
that moves among the living,
and mangled, tries to skip and play
like he did in the very beginning.

Yet his owners keep him in the family,
and try to ignore his undead fate.
Because they feel so guilty
for forgetting to close the gate.

Nightmare

Shaken
from dreams beyond my control

These witching hour moments

Greeted by an unforgiving moonlight
through heavy curtains
that split the seam
and glide
over your curves

You are still there

But,
in my nightmare—
      where my greatest fears are alive and well—
you are not

Life is precious

So precious
that sharing someone else's
can become your biggest responsibility
to be let down
means you have returned
to stardust

In this nightmare,
      I am alone
            Damned on earth

Sage and rose petal
burn within these halls
the dream catcher hangs
over our bed

But none of it works
it's not supposed to

And like miracles,
you really want them to

In those nightmares,
I am what haunts The Moyer house
maybe he's pissed we live here

Why?

We don't get upset when he roams the halls,
and makes the dog upset

In my never ending nightmare,
I am basked in a melancholy
that my literary heroes
could not prepare me for

This fate of Fortunado

This Witch House cackling

The rats laugh in the walls
            and I am without my Annabelle Lee
                        My Lenore

This Gothic fantasy
tangled into my brain
like September spider webs
in the corners of every room

In these nightmare,
the spirits I've disturbed
come to me

And stand
outside of my fiction

They run screaming through the house
as I sit in my brooding chair
with the blood-red upholstery

Your spirit
nowhere
in sight

Tonight
as I fall asleep
I'll say the same thing I say every night

Let it be a dream
within a dream
You walking through a field of poppies
*in your faded cotton dres*s

And not this haunt

Not this questionable premonition
not this object in my
third eye's rear-view mirror

A dream.
like the one that I live
with you
in this life

For Aged Poets

There is nothing more disgusting,
vile,
ugly,
and worn out,
than an aged poet

All those dead years,
spent on perfecting the art,
as they suck on cigarettes,
wine bottles,
and choke down cheap food

All those years
of wear and tear
The poor years—
          dressed in the finest
          thrift store garb.
Crawling through back alley blues—
          lacking the money,
          but spending every cent
          on the voices of the past.
                    Respecting and fearing
                    their weaponry,
                    as they learn
                    to perfect their own
                    weapons

There is nothing more
underestimated,
misjudged,
unappreciated,
and misunderstood
than an aged poet

Sign me up

Hurricane

We got along

It was the first time
since I was a child

And there I was
in the same setting:
a large work truck that I nicknamed
"The Battle Van."
(Even though it always looked more like an
ice cream truck on steroids)

It was 5 a.m.,
and we were still out
trudging from apartment to apartment
pumping water out of the basements

The hurricane had ended a few hours before

"No," he said.
"It looks like we can't go that way.
Shit, did you see that truck?
The water was up to the cab."

Most of the streets were flooded,
but the trains were still running
and we were still laughing
in central Pennsylvania

"If I had a gas-powered pump
this would go a hell of a lot smoother.
But the stores were all sold out."

The next day,
he got his gas pump
and it worked
so well
that we spent the next night
in the emergency room

This is the way
carbon monoxide poisoning
works:
there's a scale
that ranges from 0 to 40.
Over 40,
you pass out,
die

Dad was at 35
and left the hospital at midnight

My aunt told me
that he and my uncle
were in the basement
running
his brand
spanking
new
gas-powered water pump

Then the window they were using
as an exhaust port
slammed shut

And they didn't hear it close

So they emerged
from the foot of water
in the cellar
and wound up in the back
of an ambulance

But the neighborhood
is now free of carbon monoxide,
according to the fire department

And so is dad,
according to the doctor

"I'm fucking hungry,
he said
as he walked to the car
with my mother

Lamp Lighter

Last night I dreamt
that you and I
were fireflies

No electric bill
No rent
No job to drive to
No aches from sport injuries

Just fireflies
husks
and feelers,
and a blinker
that guide hitchhikers home

My grandmother told me
that it was illegal to kill them
when I was a child

I believed her

She was protecting me from
facing the fragility of
life back then

But there we were,
in the dream

A little flicker
with every bob and weave,
like a fluorescent boxer—

Graceful and together

Then I awoke
to dog kisses,
and the darkness
of winter at 6 a.m.

So, I reached for the light

War

On days like this
I miss my childhood room

The great escape

I miss my father
I miss how we didn't get along when I was growing up

He taught me how to read
He taught me how to type

I also miss pining for that certain woman
in the heat of August nights
in my empty bed

Now I have her

I miss the angst and confusion
of youth
I miss wasting my
teenage years
by being myself

Those stories now exist in memory

They exist on the page

I miss
the last time
I wept

Life is slowly making me into a
tough-enough
motherfucker

But I do not miss
the last time
that the blank page's bite
tore me in half

In my head,
I hear a bell ding

It's the next round
poet warrior

You don't own a white flag
you son of a bitch

Marriage: Side "B"

Some days
she'll come home
and bring work
with her

She chose to ignore the memos I left
which stated
that work was an unwelcomed guest
in our home

She'll become passive-aggressive
and more annoyed because she can't
get under my skin
I've become too tough
I know that this isn't
my auburn beauty

But she won't let me cleanse her

So, I'll cook dinner
while she goes crunches in our living room;
and works her legs
her abs
and her ass
I'll sneak glances
and think about how good
last night was

How she worked me like a plow horse
until she came
and almost punched a hole in the drywall

I think about that for a while
even after I'm done cooking
and she tells me that she's not eating
"That shit"

Then we'll each storm off
to our hemispheres of the house
Her half: stylish and calculated
Mine: wild and creative

She'll take the dog
and the wine glass

I'll take the typewriter
and the scotch

Then, we'll spend the night
listening for each other
her footsteps making my heart skip
the sound of the Royal making her smile

Then we'll take turns bathing,
and I'll write my poem all over the shower wall

But sometimes,
in the dead of night,
a door will unlock
and creak open

And the other will pretend
that they are asleep

Secretly anticipating love

Familiar

Flesh will always seek flesh
night and day will always
chase each other across the sky
there will be time for hopping into rain puddles
and climbing flowered hills

This is certain

Certain as a stoplight
and as noticeable as footprints
in fresh snow

But this
isn't like that

Not exactly

It's not like it used to be
especially when it's this hard

But this is fair

I like this

It's all I've ever known...

Write Right

Those who get high often,
will write about getting high often.

Those who love often,
will write about loving often.

Those who plant flowers often,
will write about planting flowers often.

Those who get sick often,
will write about sickness often.

Those who get sad often,
will write about sadness often.

Those who work too hard or too often,
will never be writers.

I like to write about the things you often forget.

Someone has to play the martyr...

Closing the House

The end of the night
is almost always the same
my wife likes to shower with me,
and loves when I read to her in bed

One paragraph
one poem
or one sentence
and she's asleep

So I go from room to room
and turn off the lights
put any wet laundry in the dryer
give the animals their food ahead of time
and contemplate the next word

Anything but sleep

Sleep is always disturbed

If I sleep on my back,
I'll have a nightmare

If I sleep on my side,
my sport injuries ache in the morning

If I sleep on my stomach,
I'll wake up without an appetite

I always sleep on my back,
at least there is a potential for fiction

She sleeps through my bumping about
and gets jealous when,
in the morning,
she learns that I chose the word
over her

Hey…
one way or another
someone is making love
to me tonight

Nature Writing

Emerson
was always boring to me
Thoreau
put me to sleep
on my parent's couch
when I was 15

I am too far removed
from reading about nature.
all I do now
is fear and respect it

I only sing of it
when there's nothing else to write

Or when I'm fishing...

Nature
should always be experienced first-hand

It knows of its own beauty
It knows it is dangerous enough
It knows that it is poetry
That's why it writes its own poetry

It knows what it is going to do to humanity
no matter how often
they sing of it

It remembers what it did to dinosaurs
nature is a beautiful woman scorned

So, I'll let her write her own autobiography
and be plagiarized by naturalists
who are searching for a voice

Like old men
in bus stations
who can't shut up
about the weather

Five Minutes

That's the most amount
of time
that I get to spend
at this machine

The tipping point...

When I don't have to answer
to anybody
or anything
   Not to police
   to arsonists
   to thieves
   to the time clock
   or khakis and ties

Even illness remains
at bay
during this time

Five minutes
to produce something
that you may never find beautiful.
but means the world to me

Until the next rolls in
on a tide
of inspiration

Five minutes
before the doors start
to rattle,
and the noises
float back

The outside world
is there again,
and as I lock
my front door,
I dream about
the next
5 minutes

Pickled

There's something about
a jar of pickled eggs
sitting under the bar top
on a wood shelf

All the men
sitting on their stools
with their whiskey
and their beer
and sometimes
this jar is opened

He reaches in with a slotted spoon
It drags against the glass
but the liquid mutes the scrape
the bartender puts the chosen one in a little dish
and slides it to the one
with the sausage fingers

He pops it in with one motion
and chews
the possibility of life
had been doomed from the start
it had been drowned in brine
and vinegar tears

I now understand
a hysterectomy
in my own way

Masked

At the tail end
of the pandemic,
I would still wear a mask
that covered all of my lower face
and, some people would tell me
"Hey, you don't have to wear that in here anymore"

I would then think
about my wife
and my newborn daughter
and how I'm not ready yet
and how I'd feel comfortable protecting them
for a while longer
and it wouldn't be that big of a deal
so I'd reply thusly

"I know,
but you see...
I have this really epic beard
under here
and it has the tendency
to make men violently jealous,
and turn women into sex-crazed maniacs

So, really...
I have this on
for your safety

No need to thank me"

Camera Roll

I become saddened
by my cell phone
for many reasons
besides addiction

For instance,
my camera roll...

When I scroll through it
back in time,
this pandemic hasn't happened yet
you take our daughter
back into yourself
and she slowly disappears
into your womb
as my hair grows back

I am so happy
to be here
in the now
with you
and her

Parenthood

It goes like this:

Kill your demons
accept your demons
embrace your demons
or tuck them deep inside
so that they only attack you
in your dreams
or in your weakest moments
of reflection

But never
Never
Let your child
Grow to love them

Wanting Relief

Legs crossed at the knees
in figure four
and scissors
legs crossed at the ankles
slouching towards oblivion
elbows resting on knees
hands cup the chin
squeezing out the restlessness
man spreading
arms crossed across the belly
legs crossed at ankles
arms crossed at wrist
hangs pinched between thighs
deep exhale

Someone at this poetry reading
has to pee

Dear Katie,

Don't even let them get to you.
They don't deserve you.
Don't give them a shred of your sadness.
Don't give them an ounce of your heartache.
Don't let them drink a drop of your tears.
You are strong;
stronger than I could ever dream of being.
You are kind;
kinder than I deserve.
You mean more than you'll ever know.
We are all lucky to know you.
Everything I do reminds me of you.
That's why I enjoy the things I do.
I know that this is cheesy.
I know you've rolled your eyes twenty times by
  now.

But sometimes poets write corny letters
to their significant other.

Thank you
for the opportunity
to do so.

Cereal Killer

Bowl of Boo Berry
TV Special on Ed Gein
October done right

Oak

In the mourning mist
The oak tree's silhouette
Attacks this old house

Aside from creative writing endeavors, Ryan J. Torres is also a teacher, editor, typewriter collector, and *Dungeons & Dragons* nerd. He has been published both nationally and internationally, and is the author of *Poem, and Other Four-Letter Words; Blessed Are the Snakes; Nylons for Parachutes*; and the horror short story collection *A Rustle in the Attic*.

Torres resides in Doylestown, Pennsylvania in a creepy house with his wife, daughter, and pets.

www.ingramcontent.com/pod-product-compliance
Lightning Source LLC
Chambersburg PA
CBHW071347090426
42738CB00012B/3043